I0620394

THE CÖLÖÜR PENCILS WÖNDER
WHAT TÖ DRAW TÖDAY.
SÜDDENLY, THEY GET AN IDEA,
LET'S DÖ MÜSIC!

RED PENCIL DRAWS A DRŰM. SŰDDENLY, IT GŐES TŐ LIFE WITH LŐŰD BŐŐM! BŐŐM!

" BLÜE PENCIL DRAWS A GÜITAR. THE STRINGS START STRÜMMING STRÜM! STRÜM!

YELLOW PENCIL DRAWS A VIOLIN. THE BOW GLIDES ACROSS SWISH! SWISH!

GREEN PENCIL DRAWS A FLŰTE.
A SŐFT MELŐDY FLŐATS TŐŐT!
TŐŐT!

Örange pencil draws a pianö. The keys start playing plink! Plönk!

PÜRPLE PENCIL DRAWS A
TRÜMPET. IT PLAYS LÖÜDLY
TÖÖT! TÖÖT!

THE CÖLÖÜR PENCILS REALIZE
THEY MADE A MAGICAL
ÖRCHESTRA!

THEY PICK UP THEIR DRAWN
INSTRUMENTS AND START
PLAYING TOGETHER BOOM!
STRUM! SWISH! TOOT! PLINK!

THEIR MÜSIC FILLS THE AIR WITH CÖLÖÜRS AND HAPPINESS!

THE MÚSIC FADES AS THEY SMILE, EXCITED FÖR THEIR NEXT ADVENTÚRE.

SAEED FOROUGHI IS A RENOWNED CANADIAN MUSICIAN, PERFORMER, AND COMPOSER. HE CONDUCTS THE RUMI ENSEMBLE AND CELTIC MEDITATION IN HALIFAX AND PLAYS CLASSICAL AND IRISH FLUTE, CELTIC HARP, SANTUR, AND SETAR. A GRADUATE OF TRINITY COLLEGE LONDON, HE WAS THE PRINCIPAL FLUTIST FOR THE PORTUGUESE SYMPHONY. SAEED HAS RECORDED AND PERFORMED ACROSS CANADA AND INTERNATIONALLY, INCLUDING TOURS IN JAPAN, ENGLAND, AND WESTERN CANADA.

FUN FACTS ABOUT THE INSTRUMENTS AND THEIR SOUNDS

DID YOU KNOW THAT EACH INSTRUMENT CREATES A UNIQUE SOUND BECAUSE OF ITS SHAPE AND HOW PLAYED?

DRUMS MAKE LOUD, BOOMING SOUNDS BECAUSE THEY ARE STRUCK WITH STICKS OR HANDS. THE LARGER THE DRUM, THE DEEPER THE SOUND!

GUITARS PRODUCE BEAUTIFUL, STRUMMING SOUNDS WHEN THEIR STRINGS ARE PLUCKED. ELECTRIC GUITARS CAN MAKE ALL KINDS OF COOL EFFECTS!

VIOLINS CREATE SMOOTH, MELODIC MUSIC WITH A BOW THAT MOVES ACROSS THE STRINGS. ONE OF THE OLDEST INSTRUMENTS!

FLUTES MAKE SOFT, SWEET NOTES WHEN AIR IS BLOWN ACROSS A HOLE. THE LONGER THE FLUTE, THE DEEPER THE SOUND!

PIANOS HAVE BLACK AND WHITE KEYS THAT PLAY DIFFERENT SOUNDS WHEN PRESSED. LIKE A WHOLE ORCHESTRA IN ONE INSTRUMENT!

TRUMPETS HAVE BRIGHT, BOLD SOUNDS THAT COME FROM BLOWING AIR THROUGH A MOUTHPIECE. YOU CAN MAKE THE NOTES HIGH AND LOW BY PRESSING THE VALVES!

EACH INSTRUMENT IN AN ORCHESTRA ADDS ITS OWN SPECIAL MAGIC TO THE MUSIC, JUST LIKE HOW EVERY COLOUR PENCIL ADDS ITS OWN COLOR TO THE WORLD!

www.ingramcontent.com/pod-product-compliance
Lightning Source LLC
Chambersburg PA
CBHW041133120626

46547CB00019B/2980